My Grandmother Loves Me

Written by Contessa Gray
Illustrated by Gaurav Bhatnagar

My Grandmother Loves Me

Written by Contessa Gray
Illustrated by Gaurav Bhatnagar

© Copyright Contessa Gray 2022

All Rights Reserved.
No part of this book may be reproduced or used in any manner without written permission of the copyright owner except for the use of quotations in a book review and certain other noncommercial uses permitted by copyright law.
This book was manufactured in the United States of America
ISBN: 978-1-959667-18-6
Pa-Pro-Vi Publishing: www.paprovipublishing.com

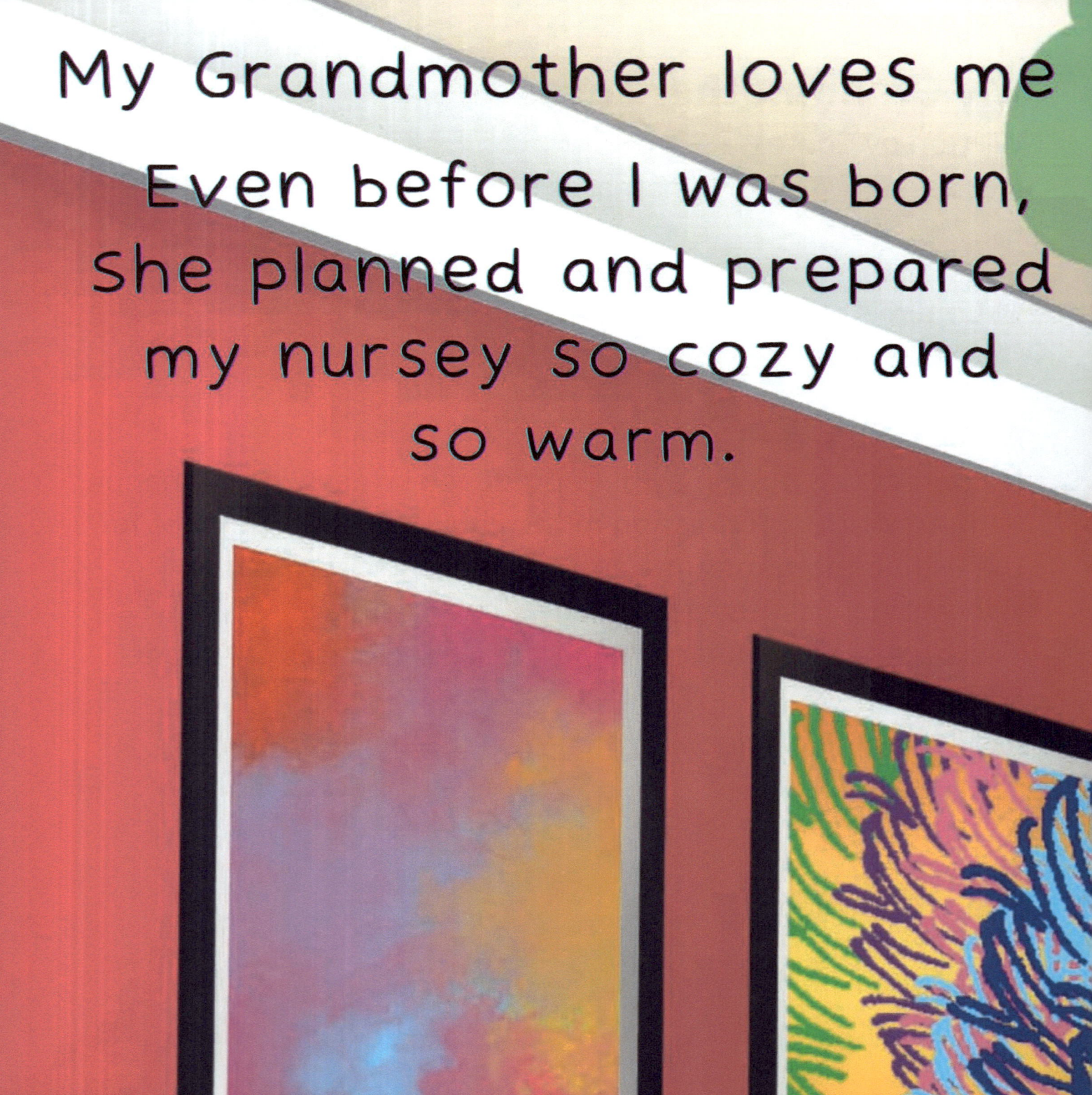

My Grandmother loves me
Even before I was born,
She planned and prepared
my nursey so cozy and
so warm.

My Grandmother loves me She paced and prayed for a safe delivery,

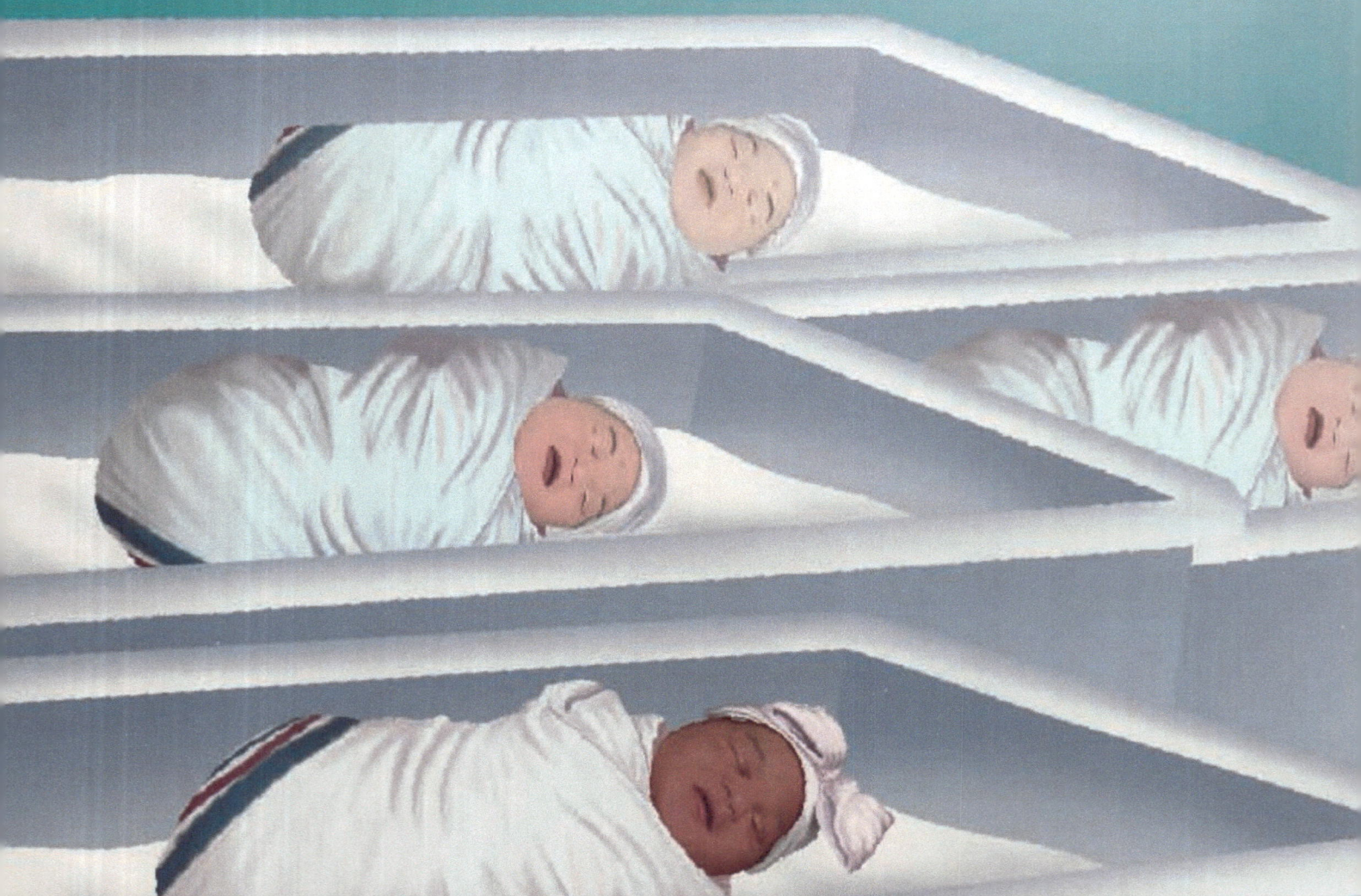

and when I popped out, I held her heart in captivity.

she loves to dress me

she loves to feed me

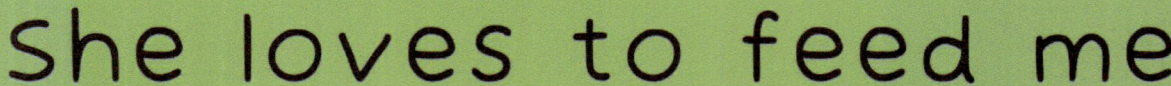

She loves to read me books
And rock me until I'm sleepy.

My Grandmother Loves me

She takes me to the zoo, she teaches me about the animals what they eat and like to do.

My Grandmother Loves Me

She takes me to the beach and pool. She puts on my beach shoes, my floaties and sunscreen too.

My Grandmother Loves me

we sing songs and dance together,

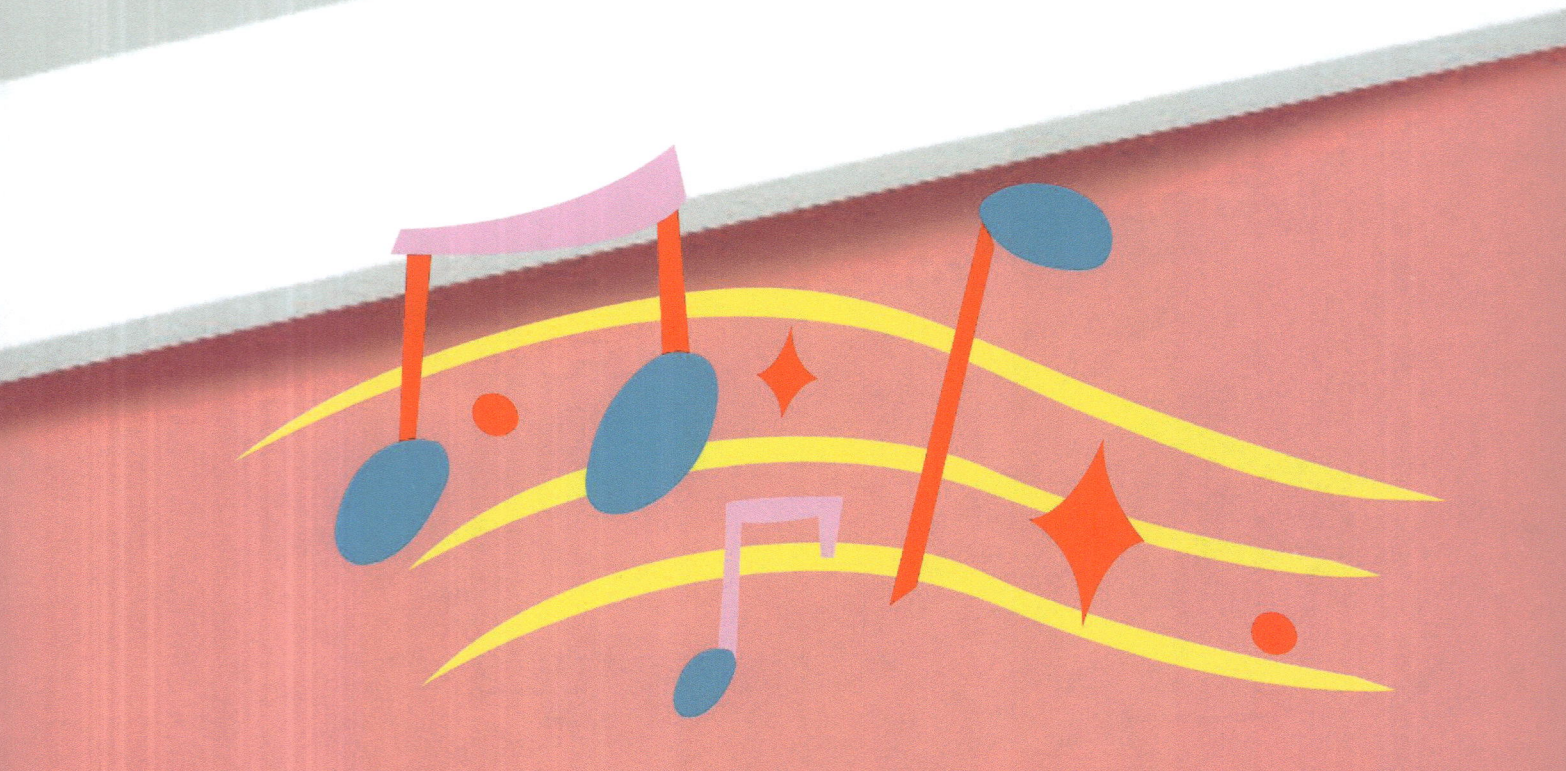

We love all kinds of music just like we love all kinds of weather.

We Gaze at the stars,
And the moon too.

She says "Any day is a good day spent with you" my Grandmother Loves me and
I LOVE HER TOO!

My Grandmother Loves Me

About the Author

Contessa has always loved caring for people professionally as a nurse for over 20 years and personally. She believes that serving those in need and those that she loves is her life purpose. Living in her purpose inspired her to embark on the journey of becoming an author to share her experiences.

To contact the author, you can email her at mehanah73@gmail.com or follow her on Facebook under Contessa M. Gray

www.ingramcontent.com/pod-product-compliance
Lightning Source LLC
Chambersburg PA
CBHW042015150426
43196CB00002B/49